"Life is not about waiting for the sto[rm]... learning to dance in the rain" - Vivia[n Greene]

## CHAPTER ONE: It all began in Portugal.

Upon seeing that quote just now, I realize that maybe that's the way I should have treated my diagnosis. Maybe I should have tried to embrace my problems and faults a lot sooner than I did. Maybe I should have turned and said "Fuck you raging hormones, I'm going to beat you". I didn't, though. I let them win. For a long time. I look back now and realize I was lost in the storm, searching for a way out...but I didn't see any light. Just dark, grey clouds and lots of cold rain, no sunlight. I can sometimes still feel the freezing rain against my skin, the feeling of darkness that clouded my young, vulnerable mind at the time, and it gives me goosebumps. I was eleven years old when it got bad. I remember feeling unsure of what was "wrong" with me. I would jump randomly, have panic attacks, etc. I was confused. I felt alone, I felt so weird. I hoped that maybe someday, somebody could give me an answer.

It happened in Portugal. I remember that day I was feeling particularly 'jumpy'. We spent most of the day by the pool, my parents sunbathing and myself and my younger brother, Callum, were swimming and jumping into the water. I ignored the twitches, thinking that it was just another day. I noticed a cute boy eyeing me up, so I managed to let it go for a while. I was wrong. That night, we went out for a meal at a Chinese restaurant. I couldn't breathe. I swear to you. It felt like..a huge weight was pressing down on my chest. I knew something was going to happen. I panicked. My mother tried to calm me down, nothing was working. I even went to the bathroom to try to calm down, but the attack only got worse. We went back to the hotel, then. Things only got worse. I felt like I was going to have a seizure and die. My mind was beginning to fog, I wanted to die. I didn't want to go through it. My dad went down and asked reception to call a taxi, that we needed to go to the hospital, and we needed to go now. I silently begged for death, as I was helped out of the hotel by my dad and into the taxi. My legs were numb..my face was numb..my breathing was shallow..my twitches were worsening..what the hell was wrong with me!?. I remember sitting in the taxi as we drove through the night, and I was never so relieved to see a hospital in my entire life.

My dad helped me into the hospital. As soon as the doctor's saw the state I was in, they pulled me into a room and jabbed an adrenaline shot into my right arm. They thought I had taken drugs. I yelped in pain, but was too upset to care at the time. My mind was so fragile, I could feel my independence being crushed by the overpowering depression I was feeling. "Take me Tessie, please"I thought. I have thought that multiple times throughout my life. My grandaunt Tessie had died that year, we had been very close. She didn't take me, though. She didn't hold my hand and take me to eternal happiness, but I could feel her there. She was holding my hand, but she just wasn't going to let me die. It just wasn't my time.

The hospital gave me multiple scans, checked my brain. There was nothing wrong..well, nothing physically wrong. I was giving up hope, to be honest. Nothing was fitting into place, nothing was helping. The memories I have of the hospital were feeling so down. My father slept on the chair beside my bed for the two nights I stayed there. He was always so supportive, and I will be forever in his debt. My brother cried in the hotel room to my mam with worry. It wasn't easy on everyone, not just me. It took me until I got out of my depressive state to realize this. Things could only get worse in my eyes. Nothing seemed to be getting better, I didn't improve for a long while. I wish that holiday had of gone better. Portugal is such a beautiful place, and I wish I had of enjoyed it more. For years I was afraid to return, but I hope to return someday and actually enjoy it. Take in the scenery. I can travel now, it's just Portugal isn't on my list right now. When my cousin Reigan and my best friend Kimberley are allowed to travel alone, we will go there together I'm sure. just Portugal isn't on my list right now. When my cousin Reigan and my best friend Kimberley are allowed to travel alone, we will go there together I'm sure. Now that I've improved greatly, I have visited Tenerife and Lanzarote and London(twice!). In Tenerife I went on a full day tour and all! In Lanzarote we only went on the half day one, but that is only because we were trying to relax and didn't want to be too sleepy! Maybe someday. I stayed with my family in London, but I managed to go to the Imperial War Museum and the Shard and the Sherlock Holmes museum (favorite!). Yes, I was slightly jumpy. But that is because London is so big, and I also have agoraphobia(a fear of large spaces). So if you or anyone you know is suffering with anxiety and struggles to go abroad, don't give up yet! If I can do it, so can you/them. After all, we are one in the same.

Just a tip. If you or someone you know is struggling with going abroad, make sure you understand that it isn't easy for yourself/them. Don't try to force yourself/them to go abroad. The time will come when you/they can do it! It's not the end of the world when you get diagnosed, though it often feels that way. Just make sure you/they get the help you/they need in order to feel comfortable enough going abroad. I find that when I am in large, open spaces I must hold onto somebody. Maybe if you/they are in a long term relationship, a boyfriend/girlfriend or whatever the person is to you/them may help! I always find that when I am in a relationship, holding hands or linking arms always does the trick! I feel more secure and my anxiety levels instantly decrease and I can finally buy those pair of shoes I've been dying to get since the previous year! Try it. This may sound embarrassing, but it helps me too. If you/they don't have a significant other, try holding onto a friends hand or a parent/sibling! Even linking arms, which seems like a more friendly gesture. My mother often links arms with her brother when we go out for family meals when he is home from London, and people don't think they are dating! Just do whatever makes you/them comfortable. It honestly helps in the long run.

While you are preparing for your holiday, maybe know in advance what you are going to do. Ask a parent/friend or whoever you are going on holiday with to make a list with you of things you will do while abroad. That way, you can prepare yourself for what is to come. Every night before bed, maybe two weeks before you go on holiday, imagine yourself in these places. Maybe one per night, if you are going for two weeks. If not, I still recommend doing this two weeks in advance. I literally just thought of this idea, and I personally think it's a good one. I wish I had of thought of it sooner, but I will be doing it before I go abroad in June 2016! Anyway, prepare yourself for the trips or poolside relaxation days. This may help your anxiety levels if you know what's coming. To parents/whoever is reading this book: I know this may seem like a bummer or hard work, but your child/friend or whoever needs it. I wish my parents had of done this kind of thing with me! I'm not saying they weren't helpful, but this would have been wonderful!

Example:

Sit down and decide with the person you will be taking this trip with where you will be going. If you are unsure, use google and look up places in, say, New York. There are a lot of things in New York that you can do. So, say you are going on a Winter trip for four days. Here's an example list.

Day 1: relaxation day, dinner at 6 O'Clock in hotel.

Day 2: Pony and trap ride through Central Park, dinner at 7 O'Clock in hotel. Walk through the city to see all the lights.

Day 3: Visit to the statue of liberty and the USS Intrepid. Dinner at 8 O'Clock in hotel.

Day 4: Shopping trip to pick up some glamorous winter clothes! Pack before dinner, then dinner at 7 O'Clock in hotel.

I hope my new idea works wonders for you all, good luck!

**Chapter Two: School.**

School. Don't we all dread it? I certainly did. Nothing ever seemed to go right in school. I was the quiet one, so I was often picked on for twitching. They would deny it now, but the girls were terrible for it. The boys in my school never laughed at me for my tourettes(well, some of them did), but more so because they were pig ignorant. When I moved to Rathangan, and started going to school, I knew I didn't belong there. A lot of people made that quite clear to me. I wanted to go back to Naas so bad. I felt so left out of everything. I presumed it was because these people had grown up together. I was never one for making friends, though. I sucked at it. Even in Naas I had only had one friend, Emma, and my cousin Reigan who didn't necessarily count as a friend because she was family. I never quite understood why I couldn't make friends. I didn't have the confidence to talk to people, that much was clear. I just didn't understand why people never approached me. I always thought "maybe there is something wrong with my appearance". Growing up, I thought I was just ugly. I didn't bother with make up until I was fourteen, while all the other girls were slapping it on every morning in primary school. I was quite behind on a lot of things. There was one thing, though. I was afraid to be *me*.

I was very into movies like Star Wars and Lord of the Rings from a very young age. By the time I made friends, none of them were interested in those movies in the slightest. That was very hard on me. Even during my 'emo' phase in secondary school, no one was interested in those types of bands except my best friend Kimberley(who I didn't meet until second year).

Things became extremely hard for me in secondary school. I would almost have panic attacks in class, until one day I did. One of my teachers yelled at me(only a little) for talking in class. I was a very good student, and it was the first time I had dared do it in her class. I felt so upset with her, she knew I was a nice, quiet girl. I began to panic. Things got worse and worse, and before I knew it I was sitting outside in the assembly area. I had to go outside for the last class with a boy I had been friends with and breathe in the fresh air. My face had become numb, I couldn't move my thumbs and my breathing was extremely shallow. Things only got worse from there. I would have a panic attack in school every single day. I was attending counselling at that stage. The women who originally worked with me were nice, but after one retired and the other left I lost interest in going. I was so stressed out that I self harmed every day. My legs were destroyed, my right arm (inside and out). I was a miserable, depressed teenage girl who hadn't a clue what was up with her.

One of the days I attended counselling, I learned that I had Tourettes syndrome, Comorbid anxiety disorder and Asperger's. Hearing that I had something was a sigh of relief. I wasn't going mad, and I wasn't dying. I was just unusual. I was just different. I stopped self harming, and I became determined to beat everything. Of course, nothing like that ever works straight away. If you or someone you love in suffering from either or all of these mental illnesses that is something you must understand. It doesn't just go away. I'm a firm believer that there is always light. You just have to look for it. If you don't see it, you're not looking hard enough. There's nothing wrong with me, and there's nothing wrong with you or the person you love. You/They are simply different.

The secondary school I was in weren't particularly helpful, either. If you find yourself in this scenario, I don't suggest leaving. I'm sure your parents will be aware. My parents were very aware that I wasn't receiving the help promised to me when I was diagnosed, and when I returned to school after my breakdown in first year. Just remember you/they are strong enough to beat this on your/their own. Of course you/they will need support, but you/they are more than capable of gaining victory on your/their own.

I suggest finding something you are very interested in. For me, that was finding out about Sherlock Holmes and the

Walking Dead and my love of Star Wars and Lord of the Rings ever since I was a child. Whenever I felt panicked or agitated about something that happened in school, I would switch on the T.V and watch one of my favorite episodes of Sherlock (so, them all basically) or turn on a Star Wars film (what is the big deal about the prequels!?). Having Asperger's means that I can watch movies multiple times in the same day, and I never EVER get bored. It's quite funny. My family find it cute. So that's basically what I done after a hard day at school.

At first, I let the bullies get to me. I'll be honest and say I cried, they have that victory. Though sweet victory was all mine when I told my mother, and she would call the school and demand they be spoken to. When I heard the words

"I'm sorry. I didn't mean it" come from their mouths, I couldn't help but chuckle in my mind and think "that's right, bitch!. I wouldn't say that, though. Not out loud, oh no. I'd say "It's fine" quietly and scamper off before I wet myself laughing at the idiots!

My mistake though, was not being strong enough to kick the living daylights out of every person who ever made a laugh at me, or passed a rude comment, or pointed as I twitched. Those people will know who they are if they read this book, but they won't. They are far too stubborn. I'm not telling you to go on a rampage and kick them all where the sun don't shine, but be strong enough to do what you want to do! Whether that be passing a comment back, or giving them a right slap outside the school gates at hometime! Be brave! Be you!

As I previously stated, I always knew I didn't belong in this town. That's why I worked hard and got into Maynooth University. I am currently studying Arts, and my subjects are Anthropology, History and Philosophy. I plan on dropping Philosophy next year as I move to the Maynooth campus(I am currently attending the Kilkenny campus) and keeping History and Anthropology. By May 2018 I will have a Bachelor of Arts degree in History and Anthropology. I then plan on moving to London to study either Egyptian Archaeology or Sociocultural Anthropology. I may even change my mind, but that's the two I want to do as of now! What I'm trying to tell you by boasting about my university degree is, don't give up. School WILL be tough. There will be bullies, and fake friends, and horrible teachers who can't teach properly. You have to stand up and say "enough! I WILL go to university and I WILL succeed!". Stick your middle finger to those teachers who say you can't do it(not literally, or you won't be going anywhere except home for life!) and get your head down and start studying! Nothing in life is easy, and having a disorder doesn't make it any easier. Yes you get privileges, like free travel passes and extra classes in school, but a free travel pass won't get you a job where you want to work! The latter does, though.

In those extra classes, pay attention. If you have a free class in school, do your homework (yes even if there is no teacher there!). Ignore your friends chattering(even the real ones). If they really wanted to do well too, they would be working like you! Don't feel like you are being rude, tell them you want to do your homework or whatever work was left for you by your teacher! If they get offended, they aren't real friends. I found this in school. The real friends done their work with me, the fake friends kept distracting me in any way they could possibly think of! I even got in trouble a few times due to a certain fake friend even though it wasn't me! Keep up with your work. That way, when you go home you can spend 2-3 hours studying instead of rushing to get your homework done or the work your teacher left which is due tomorrow morning! Don't let ANYONE get in your way. Remember, come exam time, everyone is competing for the better grade! That is the way I thought. During my exams, I kept thinking (even about my closest friends) that they were competing with me to see who would get more points in the Leaving Certificate. Don't lose track of your future!

What I done to stay focused, was thought about my parents. My dad is the only one who works. He works for Dublin

Bus. He is a fantastic driver, but his pay isn't the best in the country. My dad works extremely hard to bring income into the house. He even works over time sometimes (from about 5 in the morning until 7/8 that night!). That doesn't mean my brother and I have everything they want us to have. They often tell me they wish they had of finished school and worked harder to achieve a better life so that we could have everything. I'm not saying I don't appreciate what I have, that's just their words. Think about your future. Your husband/wife. Your children. Don't you want that mansion you saw on Facebook with everything black in it? Don't you want your children dressed in Calvin Klein and Gucci? Don't you want that Michael Kors handbag and diaper bag? WELL THEN WORK HARD. In the words of Shia LaBeouf "Just do it!".

Another thing is university. It's easy to fall victim to bullying there, too. Don't think for one second that universities are different. Make sure you enter with a strong head. Feel proud of yourself for having accomplished what you have. You are a mature, university student! You have beat your past difficulties and are now on your way to a better, more successful life! If you are already a University student like me and are having difficulty getting along with people, don't worry about it. You don't *need* friends. You don't *need* people to like you. If you have friends outside university who are loyal to you like I do, then don't worry about it! People can be pig ignorant at times, and that's something we just have to accept. Not everyone plays fair. If you don't have friends outside University, I would suggest joining a club or society within your university. There you can meet people with common interests and perhaps make a beautiful friendship (and if you're lucky, a relationship with that hot guy/gal you have been eyeing up!). Don't lose who you are, though, just to make friends. You are unique and wonderful!

**Chapter Three: About Asperger's.**

Okay. So this chapter is for the newbies who just found out they are in our little clan. This chapter will focus on Asperger's Syndrome. If you or anyone you know has Asperger's, keep reading. Even if you/they are not newly diagnosed, keep reading. You may find out something new!

My experience with Asperger's hasn't been entirely negative. I only have it mildly. The definition of

Asperger's syndrome on AutismIreland.ie is "AS is a complex brain disorder and is seen as part of the Autistic Spectrum. Generally those affected by the condition have an IQ within the normal range but may have extremely poor social and communication skills. Common characteristics can be a lack of empathy, little ability to form relationships, one-sided conversations and an intense absorption with a special interest. Sometimes movements can be clumsy. However, with the proper support people with AS can lead full and productive lives". So in other words, Asperger's is a social disorder, it is considered in the Autistic spectrum, people who have Asperger's syndrome may find it extremely difficult to understand emotions or show empathy, they can struggle to form relationships and they can become overly obsessed with particular things (which is okay, by the way, don't be afraid of it).

For me, I find it extremely hard to form good, solid relationships with people. Friendships are very hard for me, especially. I am very quiet, so people also take advantage of me and use me for stuff. This is not a good thing, and maybe with more life experience I will learn to stop this from happening. I remember being young and being told by people that I didn't show emotion enough. Even my parents (who didn't know at the time) thought I didn't love them and that's why I sometimes acted so cold towards them. This is not the case. I know love, I can feel it. I just can't show it. If someone you know has Asperger's syndrome, you need to take this into account. If it's, for example, your daughter, you mustn't turn to her and say "Stacey we know you don't love us!" if you get into an argument about how messy her room is and she shows no emotion. This is completely normal. I know it hurts. I can feel my parents hurt at times. I can't bring myself to show them how sorry I feel, and I often feel saying sorry is not enough. I often stay in my bedroom, even in my University house. I wish I had the confidence at times to join my housemates in the living room, but I often feel unwanted. Because of my Asperger's, I don't have a bond with them like they have with one another. Only two of them know I have a disorder as of now. I feel like it's too late to let them know, so don't do that. If you are in university and have to live away from home, make sure to tell your housemates you have Asperger's. This counts if you have any other disorders too. Make sure you let them know. It's very important so that they can keep an eye on you and make sure they communicate with you because they will know you can't. Try it!

If you are still in school, it's important that you let your friends know. Maybe not your classmates, as this is none of their concern. Your teachers should know, also. I think that's very important. My school knew, therefore they told my teachers. Even though my school didn't do much, it was helpful that the teachers knew so that they could associate with me on some level and not ask me questions or to read in class(this also had to do with my anxiety and Tourettes). While my fake friends also knew I had Asperger's and other disorders, they could at least appreciate me and not ask me why I wasn't very good at communicating.

How do you tell people, you ask? Well presuming you're in school and it's your friends, you just sit with them at lunch and tell them. All it takes is a little courage to say "I have Asperger's syndrome" and if you have other disorders, mention those too. Make sure to focus on whichever one you are most concerned about. They are bound to be unsure of what Asperger's is, so make sure you know yourself and tell them. Maybe just say "It's a social disorder. It means that I can be a little cold sometimes, and I find it difficult to understand body language and that's why I can be a little quiet". If they make a joke of it, ditch these friends right away. I'd rather be alone than hang out with fools like that! Remember, your disorder is a part of you. While it shouldn't control your life (remember: "I have Asperger's, but Asperger's doesn't have me!"), it is there. If they laugh at your Asperger's, they are laughing at you! You don't need this negativity in your life, no one does. I'm sure your friends will be understanding, even the fake ones. My fake friends were understanding, yet I haven't heard from them since I left school. It's important to mention it to your friends, as they may misunderstand you or think you don't want to be their friend. If you are concerned about telling your teachers or principle at school, ask a parent/guardian to do it for you. This should be done, anyway. If you were diagnosed by a doctor or psychiatrist, make sure to have a letter from them to your school stating that you have Asperger's(and whatever else). Your school can therefore keep this in your medical record and if they are any bit decent, will take care of you properly and take your disorders into consideration. I'm not sure about other countries, but in Ireland people with Asperger's are awarded extra classes in school. Take these if they are awarded in your country. It is a great help and you will get extra help. Especially if it is one on one. You may feel more comfortable asking your teacher in these private lessons questions you had in class.

If you are in University, make sure to let the head of your university know. In my university in Kilkenny, we don't have a dean. We just have a president, and she let all my lecturers know that I has Aspergers, Tourettes and anxiety. When I go up to Maynooth, I will have to inform my new lecturers of my disorders. I suppose there's not really a need to. In Kilkenny, there's only about 20 of us in a classroom sized room. We don't have any lecture theatres, so it's easy for the lecturers to spot me and ask me a question or to read a passage (which is a big no-go area for me). I still suggest letting them know, though, even if you have a massive lecture theatre. This can give you access to things like extra time doing assignments (if needed ONLY) and recorder pens and such. I have a problem paying attention in class, so when I go to Maynooth the MAP office (Maynooth Access Program, in particular the disability office. I'd suggest talking to one of these people if you have them in your country), they will give me said pen and I will get better supports than I do in Kilkenny. I can even attend counselling sessions if I feel like it, or if I hit a bad time in my life again. The way it works in Maynooth is you don't really have to attend counselling on set dates. If you're feeling particularly down and need someone to talk to, you can arrange a session with the counsellor. You don't necessarily have to go back, unless she/he is concerned about you. If these supports are available to you, I'd suggest taking them. Besides giving you access to these supports, it can also give you a sense of relief that someone understands why that essay is late or why you left class early. Just give it a try!

**Eye Contact**

Eye contact is really difficult for me, and for most people with Asperger's syndrome. When I talk with people, I find it hard to look them in the eye. This can aggravate some people who don't know I have Asperger's, which is part of the reason I avoid talking to people I don't know too well.

If you are starting up a conversation with someone new and they become annoyed by the lack of eye contact, maybe tell them you have a social disorder and you can't help it. You don't have to go into too much detail, as it's not necessary for people you don't know to know this about you. If you are talking to a friend, make sure they know you have Asperger's so they don't become offended. I know it's just a little thing, but I've had boyfriends tell me I need to look into their eyes more when talking to them, and daring me to have staring contests. Which made me really uncomfortable, as you could imagine.

**Obsessions.**

With the obsessions, don't be afraid of them. Not unless they are extremely bad. My current obsessions as I write this book are Star Wars(well, I always was obsessed with that), Sherlock, The Walking Dead and The Lost Boys. All films, I know. I have a thing about movies. I love to watch them because I can bond with the characters. I suppose this is a healthy obsession, because I love to be able to understand how the characters are feeling. This actually helps me to show my emotions better, because if I see a happy couple in a film I smile, and at sad moments I cry. If you are feeling like your obsession is wrong, don't. This is part of who you are. Even if you are obsessed with collecting pens, there is nothing wrong with that. Collect all those pens!

If someone you love is going through an obsessive stage with something, for example, the pens, don't worry about it.

This is absolutely nothing to worry about. As I stated, I watch Star Wars over and over. As a matter of fact, the night before I wrote this chapter I watched "Return of the Jedi" four times! This is natural for a person with Asperger's, they don't see anything wrong with it. They shouldn't, and neither should you. My parents find my obsessions adorable, because it's unusual and it's something they haven't experienced before.

**Food.**

Food can be a big problem for people with Asperger's. I haven't suffered all to much with food. I try everything (except meat and fish as I am a vegetarian), but before that I tried almost all foods except seafood. The only seafood I ever liked was Tuna, and then again, I didn't like it all too much. If someone you know is struggling to eat different foods, that's fine too. Let them eat the same dinner every day if that's what they want. Some people with Asperger's are completely comfortable with that.

My brother also has mild Asperger's. As a child, he struggled with food and still does at some points. I remember my nana asking him if he wanted some of her famous stew, to which he would say "no". Simply because he didn't like the word! Then she would ask him if he wanted casserole. He liked that word, so he would say "yes". He didn't know that he was actually eating stew. If you have young children in your home that don't eat certain foods, it may be because they don't like the word being used. I'd suggest testing out different words and using that word at dinner time. Say you were making a stew, try using casserole like my nana did, or soup. Your young child won't know the difference, and will eat it up no problem. For me, I don't like my gravy touching anything except my potatoes. My brother can't stand mixing his food. If my mother made him a chicken curry, she would have to put his chicken and sauce on one side of the plate, and the rice on the other. He would then eat the sauce and chicken, then the rice. I also absolutely refuse to eat dinner (or any meal) without a beverage. This can be awkward for me if I am at another person's house, so I make sure to let them know in advance. If your child has a playdate, I'd suggest telling the parent's of their friend that they have Asperger's and that they don't like their food touching or to use certain words when addressing food. I know it's awkward, but it has to be done. If you are a teenager or if you are an adult, make sure to let your friends know that you need a drink while eating or you don't like your food touching. It saves you the trouble of not eating it and making them feel like it doesn't taste good or you don't like it.

## Making friends.

It's very difficult to make friends as a person with Asperger's at any age. It's even difficult for me, still. This section may not be so useful. I suppose I will tell you how I managed to become friends with my best friend Kimberley. Kimberley had no friends in school, and I noticed this once I returned to school in 2$^{nd}$ year. I decided I wanted to approach Kimberley, but I wasn't sure how. I had already had one friend(a fake one) and I knew Kimberley was a nice girl. So I went on Facebook and added her as a friend. She accepted and I seen she had a photo of Yugi Moto from Yu-Gi-Oh as her profile photo. I had liked that show as a child, so I messaged her and said "oh! You like Yu-Gi-Oh!?" and she said "yes I do". I presumed by her short reply she thought I was another bully, so I left the messages.

How I properly started was in music class. Kimberley was standing beside me as we sang a song. Our teacher was pretending to be a conductor (sorry Miss, not quite). I leaned in to her and said "you're a good singer" mid song. She smiled at me and said thanks. I knew I had made her day. From then on, I invited her to sit with me in class because she usually sat alone. One day, I invited her out to go shopping on a Saturday. I had no idea, but that was her birthday. She has told me numerous times that she was so delighted, and she ran in the door once she got home from school and cried to her mam saying she finally had a friend. I know that's probably how most people with Asperger's would react. Kimberley is the only friend who has stuck by me and has calmed me down numerous times during panic attacks and always taken my side in friends arguments. Why? Because she's a true friend. I know they're hard to find, but you will find one. You have to keep searching. I was lucky enough to find my friend soulmate at fourteen, not all of us are. Just know that if you have friends who you don't think are loyal, that you will find your true friend someday. It takes a lot of time and practice for those with Asperger's to make friends. Just know that you can do it! Believe in yourself. If you see a girl in class that you think looks friendly, or who liked your post about Star Wars, you go and talk to her! If you see that boy who you know likes Minecraft, you talk to him! I know it seems difficult. I have felt the thumping heart, the tingling tummy. I know exactly how it feels! It's worth it though when you finally have someone your own age on your side who isn't a relative!

If someone you know is struggling to make friends, make sure you give them that little push. By little push, I don't mean shove. I mean a gentle nudge every now and then.

Say things like "hey Betty, isn't that the girl from your class who likes X-Men? Yeah? Why don't you ask her to go see the new film with you this weekend?". It's always nice to know someone shares the same interests as you, but as a person with Asperger's, it's definitely not easy to make friends. The person you know feels..I can't even explain how they feel when they go to talk to someone. It's definitely worth helping them out!

Just go for it! You could end up meeting an amazing friend!

**Dating.**

Oh boy, he's/she's hot! Ever thought that? Of course you have! Then you realize you have Asperger's and you can't talk to them..am I right? Before you know it, they're gone and their number is NOT in your phone where it belongs.

I'm no good at approaching strangers like that, but I know a lot of people are. It makes me admire them in a sense (not if they're doing it every 5 minutes, though!). I admire people like that because they're not asking you out on Facebook. I like the thought of "Hey, you're pretty. I've seen you in class. Want to catch a movie with me on Saturday? Cool! Can I have your number?". To me, this sounds just great. In school as a teenager, you are going to encounter several hot boys/girls. You're going to want to ask for their number. The only way I could ever talk to a boy in my school was if I talked to him via Facebook. Literally the next day, he couldn't get a word out of me!

Some boys are definitely NOT worth mentioning, but I have had my fair share of relationships. Each one of them has known about my issues, and have taken advantage of them. I had one boyfriend who became so controlling I stopped talking to my family and had to delete my Facebook account! That is not something you want to encounter as a person with Asperger's. I'd say the dude done research on how to control a girl with Asperger's, I swear! He was that insane! My advice to people who have just started dating a new person is to wait a while before you tell them about it. Unless you guys were friends for minimum 3 months before your relationship, it's a no go. I know what you're thinking. I've thought it myself when my mam gives me advice about my relationships. "But she doesn't know him/ her!". Perhaps I do, perhaps I don't. What I can tell you, though, is that it could be a big mistake. When I told my ex boyfriends about my disorders, I didn't think they would do what they done. Why? Because I didn't know them that much! I rushed into things, and didn't give it time for them to show their true colors! So my tip to you is to wait it out. If this boy/girl seems legit and treats you right without knowing, then tell them. If they get offended and ask why you never told them, clearly tell them that you were too embarrassed. I feel this is too important to skip. Wait to see what this person is like, then explain to them. You don't want to end up being used! How to tell them? The best thing to do is to be straight forward. If you want to tell them when the conversation runs out on Facebook, that's fine too! I guess what I'm trying to say is: Don't tell people until you trust them. With fake friends it's different. You'll have known them, and of course waiting a while is also important with new friends. You can't just jump in their face and say "My favorite color is blue, by the way, I have Asperger's!". That's the improper way of doing it in any situation. Make sure you trust them even a tiny bit. You wouldn't tell your enemy your biggest secret, right? Then why tell them this?

**Sleep.**

Finding it hard to sleep at night? Same. A lot of the time I find it extremely hard to sleep. As I write this, it 's 05:56 am! I haven't slept a wink, and I'm up for Christmas dinner early tomorrow! My advice to those who are struggling to sleep, is to do something that makes you sleepy. I was just lying in bed until now, trying to sleep. Looking at the computer screen usually makes me feel tired. I don't know why, I once heard the brightness actually keeps people awake usually. Anyway, what I'm saying is read a book, watch a film, listen to a sea soundtrack or another relaxing CD. Even if it means meditating and relaxing your body to make you fall asleep, do it! Sleep is very important. I always struggled with my sleep. I remember getting up for school feeling wide awake even though I had only had two hours sleep. I'd be as alert as I was with 8 hours sleep and would get all my work done. This was in primary school. In secondary school, my sleep patterns improved because I was a teenager who was always tired. Now as I enter into adulthood, I don't feel tired as often. I struggle to get out of bed for University sometimes, but that is simply because I had a lack of Vitamin B12 in my body from being a vegetarian.

If someone you know is having trouble sleeping, try the above steps. If they don't work, maybe ask their doctor for some sleeping pills. Sleeping pills didn't work on me as a child, either did Lavender. I stayed awake and my body fought off the pills. Sometimes, kids will do this. I used to get out of bed and play with my toys or draw until 6 in the morning, then hop into bed for two hours. I remember I used to wake my Mam up all the time and she used to be so mad. I don't blame her, I was up until all hours! At one point I stayed awake for two nights. Looking back I don't know how I managed it. Even though I'm struggling to sleep again, I will still take a nap during the day for an hour if I feel too tired.

Maybe if you struggle to sleep, take naps during the day. I'm not sure how a lack of sleep can affect your health in the long run (I honestly don't want to know either), but I'm sure it can't be good. If you feel drowsy, lie in bed and sleep. Even if you feel like napping on the carpet, do it! If you can get yourself to sleep do it by all means! Even if it's on the carpet or at the kitchen table! I know it makes you look like a three year old taking naps during the day, but don't think about that. Think about your health in the long run. I even nap around my friends sometimes, I don't see the big deal or what the problem is. They just shrug, say okay and continue to text or play a game on my Xbox. So the tip is: TAKE A NAP WHENEVER YOU NEED TO!

**Understanding body language.**

If there's one thing I have improved on after my diagnosis with Asperger's, it's understanding body language. Yes, I still feel awkward when I am being offered a hug, but I'm getting there. If someone wants to hug you, they will open their arms generally, am I correct? For me, it takes a minute for my body to understand what this person is doing. So someone is coming at me with their arms wide, wanting to hug me. They're also puckering their lips. I always used to find it difficult to know which cheek they were going to kiss. I was tensed up, and would mess up. What I suggest you do if you have this issue, is to watch them. If your aunt Betty is coming at you with her lips puckered out and her arms wide, respond by doing exactly what she is doing (with your arms, not your lips). Open your arms, and feel the loving hug (and the sloppy kisses, ew). Watching people in social situations also helped me. Trust me, no one is going to notice (as long as you don't gawk). Just make it less obvious. It's important that people have social skills in life, even if they're only amateur until you're 70. Try to learn by watching other people. Even ask a parent/guardian to help you out! Act out scenarios before you go on that dreadful visit to aunt Betty's house. Ask a parent/guardian to act like aunt Betty, and you obviously act like yourself, and see how it goes. Keep doing it until it's perfect (or at least until you yourself are happy with it!).

If someone you know is struggling to understand body language, make sure you act out some scenarios with them. This could help them a lot! Tell them what they should and shouldn't do in certain situations. I remember I was so quiet in primary school in Naas that when a girl in my class walked by me one day and said hello, my mam thought I didn't say hello back. I did, I just said it too low for anyone to hear. Tell them to speak up when they talk, even if it's just barely audible. At least someone can hear them! I still talk like this, though I have started to talk a little louder. I am only really loud with my best friend Kimberley. I'd say she's the only person (apart from my family) who has heard me laugh like a hyena and tell dirty jokes. Seriously!

Another problem people with Asperger's encounter is understanding sarcasm and jokes. I am absolutely terrible for this, to this day! Sometimes, people in my college dorm pull pranks on one another and I take them seriously. This one time **(PREPARE FOR COLLEGE TALK)**, a guy walked into the kitchen where I was sitting and told my friend, her friend and I that another guy was playing with himself (ew) in the living room. I took it so seriously, and was so disgusted! I was thinking "in public!?". Then it turned out to be a joke. I didn't even think that it could have been a joke. Another time, another guy I live with put dirty video's on in another guy's room. I thought it was seriously him having sexual intercourse with someone. That turned out to be a joke, too! So you see, people with Asperger's tend to not understand when something is a joke or someone is joking. This can cause people to be offended. That's another reason why it's important for friends to be aware you have Asperger's. I can't really tell you how to understand sarcasm better, because to be honest that's something I'm still struggling with. I cannot stress enough how important it is for friends to know, though. All my friends know. They don't get offended, they simply tell me they were joking and laugh. Then I understand and laugh. Asperger's logic sucks at times!

**Delayed motor skills.**

Oh Lord. Here is where I have to tell you guys how I eat my dinner isn't it? Well I don't mind if it's beneficial to you guys. I generally eat my dinner wrong. I can't use a knife properly. My hands can't seem to grasp it. My hand sort of bends when I use a fork. I bite my spoon or fork when I eat with it. When I was younger it was a lot worse, though. I used to bite my fork/spoon and drag the food off with my teeth. This is NOT good for your teeth. If you or someone you know does this, try to get them to stop. It's fine to bite the fork/spoon, just make sure to release and take the food normally. I also drink from the side of my mouth, which isn't good either because I usually spill my drink all over myself. I am trying to train myself to drink from in front. If you or someone you know does this, make sure you train yourself to drink from the front. It won't be very nice when you spill your drink all over your favorite new dress! If you attend therapy, I would suggest talking to your therapist about this. Maybe they can arrange for you to meet with an occupational therapist and they can help you out!

Also, if you are struggling with balance. I find that I struggle with balance a lot. I just fall over at random points and bump into people I didn't realize I was walking towards. If you or someone you know is struggling with their balance, Occupational therapists can also help with that! I remember I went to see one, but I was only with her a few weeks so it didn't help too much. Arrange for yourself/the person you know to see one in your area. It could be very beneficial to you! My therapist gave me some exercises (like lying down and making myself be straight, bouncing on an exercise ball without falling over, holding on to one foot). I'd suggest trying some of these at home before you book your appointment just to see how it goes for you. If they work and your balance is improving, do some research into some more exercises and choose which ones you'd like to do. If nothing improves, I'd definitely suggest booking an appointment with an Occupational therapist or asking your therapist is there any available where she/he works that she/he could talk to. If they try to cut your appointments short or if it's over within a few weeks, it's worth investing in a private Occupational therapist. This one may benefit you more, but I'd at least try to speak with one if you have free healthcare(in Ireland they are known as the HSE).

If you are a parent/guardian and your toddler has just been diagnosed with Autism/Asperger's, you may notice late developments like walking or talking. I think I was 18 months when I started to walk, and 14 months when I started to talk. This is normal for a baby with Autism. If things don't improve, maybe try bringing them to speech therapy. This way they can learn in their own time and may not have to attend a special school due to the help of the therapist. It's better to invest in this than have your child not be able to speak. If your country has free therapy, take it. Especially if it's recommended by your doctor.

**Last tip on Asperger's: DO WHAT YOU LIKE!**

A lot of the time, people are going to find you strange. Take it from me. There's certain things I find amusing or cool that other people wouldn't. I can't think of one person in my secondary school who enjoyed Star Wars as much as I do, I don't know if any of them like it at all! What's important is that you play whatever role you want to play. If you feel comfortable staying in, watching Netflix and writing stories on Quotev that's fine! If you want to go to a party and sit in the corner, that's also fine! If you want to go out and get drunk, that's fine! Just remember, do what you like. Don't feel like you can't do something just because you have Asperger's syndrome. I remember being 14-16 years old and believing when I was 18 I wouldn't go out and party. I go out in college every now and then (it's not really my scene, but it's different). Yes I sometimes sit there on my phone. I'll only get up and dance if the dance floor is packed, but I'm still there. I'm still listening to the music and enjoying myself. Just in my own little way. People might find it strange that I'll buy myself a West

Coast cooler, sip on it for a few minutes and not finish it, but I don't care. Quite frankly, I don't give a damn. That's the way I like to go out and party. Just because I'm not getting full blown drunk, doesn't mean I'm not having fun. I'll sit there texting people on Facebook and I'll listen to the latest charts as they blast through the stereo. The only not so fun part for me is the walk home, or when someone shatters a glass.

Do whatever makes you happy! You don't have to be like everyone else. You don't have to fit in. I never did, and I'm quite happy with that. If you're not, you need to start thinking that you are an individual person. If you want to travel the world before you're 30, you do that! If you want to go to University and study law, you do that! You work hard and you can achieve whatever you want. Remember, just because you have Asperger's, that doesn't mean you automatically can't do what you want. Do you think for one second that I thought I'd get into University? No, I didn't. I cried because I thought I wouldn't get in. I DID! That's when I realized I could do anything if I put my mind to it! I have Asperger's, but Asperger's doesn't have me! Think of this all the time. You are you..you are UNIQUE. I hope this chapter helped you. If you struggle with Tourette's syndrome(just tics), keep reading!

**Chapter Four: Tourette's Syndrome.**

Tourette's isn't the one I struggled with the most, but it is close second. I found it extremely difficult to grasp that I had this syndrome. It really is a tough one. If I were to put Tourette's into my own words, I would define it as "a neurological disorder that causes someone to twitch, jump or yell involuntarily. These movement are called 'tics'". I always found this one so embarrassing before. I don't have vocal tics, I never really did. I don't shout when I get them, I maybe just clear my throat. I don't quite understand the vocal Tourette's, I'm sorry.

**Types of Tics.**

The types of tics that come with having Tourettes are as follows:

1. Vocal.
2. Motor.

We will be focusing on the motor tics. Some motor tics include jerking your head, blinking, twitching your body, rolling your eyes back, twitching your nose and nodding. Tics I have personally suffered with are twitching my body, rolling my eyes back and nodding. Tourette's is a hard one to conceal, but we will work on that later. It's very embarrassing when you have Tourette's, isn't it? In school, I found it very hard to cope. Especially since I was the first student they had ever had to have Tourette's syndrome. They were very unhelpful, and used that as their excuse. I don't see how it's an excuse..they should have tried a lot harder to make me feel more comfortable in the school. Make sure you fight for your rights.

**School and bullying.**

School, of course, is a place of bullying. Bullying can happen for many reasons, not just to people who have a disorder. You can even be bullied if you say the wrong thing at the wrong time. Bullying comes in all forms, and I'm sure you readers know them. If you or someone you love is being victimized in school, make sure you tell a teacher, a counsellor, or a friend. If their/your friends know and aren't doing anything about it, they may not be the people to talk to. I suggest talking to a principal/headmaster about your troubles. If he/she does something about it and the bullying stops, that's wonderful! You've beat them! If he/she does something about it (or doesn't) make sure to get the police involved. The police have helped me a lot. I have been a victim to bullying quite a bit throughout my life because I'm quiet. This one girl picked on me for an entire year, then I found out my cousin knew her mother. So over he popped and talked to her, gave her a warning, and everything stopped.

If the police doesn't seem to scare them away, talk to your family members about it. Maybe get your parents/guardians to have a word with their parents/guardians. I know the police didn't work for me that time, but the policemen working at that time were pretty useless in my opinion(the ones working now are better!).

This one time I was with an ex and an old friend in the park, when I felt something sharp hit my back. I had noticed a few school dropouts hanging around, but took no notice to them. It began to throb, and I looked down to see that one of them had thrown a huge rock at me. Had that hit me in the head? I was dead. I'll admit I made myself look weak and cried. I went to the police station, and reported him for assault. He was underage, so I'm pretty sure he just got community time or something. The policeman asked me did I want him to write me a formal apology, and I declined this offer. Always decline it. It won't make you feel better, because it's just fake. If the person who is bullying you is truly sorry, they will say it to your face without being told.

I know it's sometimes hard to forgive and forget. There's some people I will just never 100% forgive. There's some things so engraved in me that I won't forget them. That doesn't mean you can't move on. Yes, your mind will wonder back sometimes. Don't let this bother you. You know that embarrassing moment where you peed your pants in public as a child and when you think about it you cringe? Yes, it's a little bit like that. It'll always come back into your mind, but you will feel nothing towards it eventually(except maybe a little embarrassment). What I mean though, is you won't be hurt by it anymore or angry. Maybe you'll just laugh it off and say "what a pathetic person". It's always better for you to get rid of negative people in your life. They cause negative energies. I always find with my Tourette's that people would make me angry just to see me twitch. This I didn't realize until later, but I know who they are and I'll always remember how they treated me.

For those of you going through bullying, I know it hurts. I've felt that pain myself. That girl I mentioned earlier used to stand outside my house she wanted to beat me that bad! You often think "why me? I didn't do anything!" Or if they are laughing at you "why do they find my pain funny?". I'll tell you why they find it funny: they're nasty people. You're going to encounter many of these people while living with Tourettes. All you have to do is learn to let go. Instead of freaking out at them, count to ten in your head and breathe normally. This way, the tics may subside. If you feel ten is too long, count to five. Once you feel calm, walk away and allow yourself to forget.

If someone you know is being bullied in school due to their Tourette's, tell their principal. Whether you are a friend, parent, guardian, sister or whatever. It doesn't matter, make sure the situations get reported. I wouldn't have gotten anywhere if my mam hadn't of constantly rang the school demanding the bullies got into trouble. If the bullying is happening outside school, as mentioned above talk to the police if talking to their parents doesn't work. If the police don't scare the person, try the opposite way around. Usually, people stop when the police get involved because of the warnings. They become afraid of what their parents will think or say or do, but in the rare cases people don't care and continue to bully.I was unfortunate to have encountered one of these bullies. I am thankful to my cousin for having a word with her mother that day! Whatever the cost, protect the person you know from bullies.

I always find that meditation helps to calm my tics, especially when I'm annoyed. Just find a nice, calming YouTube video on meditation and follow their instructions. It'll take a while for your body to be able to relax and forget about your Tourettes for, say, the thirty minutes of the video. Don't give up. I love to meditate, it makes me feel super relaxed and free. When I wake up, I don't tic for a long time because my body is so relaxed. Try it, it may be worth your while!

**Calming your tics.**

As mentioned above, I always find that the best way to calm my tics is to meditate. If this isn't your thing, and you would prefer to do something else, here are some possible ways. Remember, you c

1. If you also suffer with anxiety, anxiety attacks can often make your tics worse. When went to therapy, the one and only useful tip they taught me was how to manage an anxiety attack. Place your hands on your tummy and sit on the side of your bed. Breathe in through your nose deeply, and out through your mouth. Concentrate on the movement of your tummy. This can help relax you a lot.
2. Get a stress ball. If your tics are brought on by stress, maybe try out a stress ball. This isn't something I try. I don't often get stressed. Make sure you try this one out at least.
3. Take your medication. This seems like a no- brainer, but I often forget to take my Abilify. I will talk more about this medication later, but make sure you take it. If medications are prescribed to you, ALWAYS take them no matter what. Even if you are going out

to dinner, take it before you leave. If you feel you have to take it at a certain time and at that time you will be in the restaurant and will feel uncomfortable, take it in the loo or sneak it while you are taking a sip of water.

4. Do something that makes you feel comfortable. This is sort of similar to the stress ball. If that makes you feel comfortable do it. What makes me feel comfortable is moving my leg really fast. This one sounds weird, but when I was born my toes were bent so whenever my Tourette's gets bad, I bend my toes the way they were in the womb. Whatever it is, you can do it. Don't feel embarrassed, make sure YOU are the one feeling comfortable, no matter how odd it seems.

If you are reading this book for someone you know, make sure you are there for them when their tics get bad. They need your support at these times. If the person you know who has Tourette's is, say, in a busy shopping mall and gets nervous and starts ticing: leave or bring them to the bathroom to calm down. Don't act like they are inconveniencing you. They simply cannot help it. If you choose to bring them to the bathroom, make sure you have either their medication, a stress ball or the instructions on the breathing exercises either written down or in your head. The person who is struggling with their tics will thank you later, as they will be too stressed to think of how to do this themselves. Keep at them to do it. Whether it be sitting on the toilet seat and breathing calmly, or squeezing the stress ball tighter. It's a lot of hard work, but remember that this person needs you right now.

**Alcohol.**

With Tourettes, I have noticed that when I drink alcohol, my tics get worse. If you are experiencing this, I'd suggest not drinking alcohol when you are out. I know this seems horrible and like I am telling you what to do, but it's better. I only really drink alcohol at Christmas or in the comfort of friends and family who know of my disorder. It's up to you, but I feel really upset when I tic in public due to just having one simple drink. Even a few sips can send my tics mad. Just be careful. Maybe if you're out, order a non-alcoholic beverage. I have noticed that sugar also drives my tics mad though.

**Sweets and sugary foods.**

Urgh. This is the worst part. I absolutely adore sweets and sugary foods. I love to have two spoons of sugar in my tea, and I am obsessed with chocolate. I try my best not to eat it that much. When I do, my tics go through the roof and I feel so horrible in myself. I remember the first panic attack I ever had was aged 7, and I started ticing. All I had was one of those normal sized bags of Haribo. My mam blamed the sugar when that night I was ticing (we didn't know at this stage) and ended up nearly passing out. Imagine that. Little 7 year old me was awfully confused that night. The funny part? I had never reacted to sweets like this before! I still to this day find it so strange how sugar reacts like that in our bodies so suddenly. I ate sweets all the time as a child, and my body chose that night to react like that. I still don't understand how it works, but whatever. Just know to make sure that if you have this reaction after eating sugary foods, that you eat them in moderation. You don't have to stop completely, just cut it down if you eat a lot of them. You'll thank me in the long run!

For parents/guardians..please for the life of me make sure you enforce rules for sweets on your child with Tourette's! I don't mean to crash the party, but it's so important to make sure they don't eat too much sugar. It's not good for anyone, and it's especially not good for someone with Tourette's. If your child isn't showing any signs of distress or if their tics aren't made worse by sugar, then there is no need to worry.

**Telling people.**

It's a basic fact that people will have already guessed you had something. If you are just recently diagnosed and are still confused about it yourself, I would research any questions you may have or ask your doctor or psychiatrist.

I found it very useful when my psychiatrist gave me these stacks of papers all pinned together. I read over them a lot until I fully understood what Tourette's was. So step 1 in telling people you have Tourette's is to UNDERSTAND IT YOURSELF. Make sure you can answer any questions people may have about your disorder. I'll admit, Tourette's is an embarrassing one. Whenever I go to tell a new friend I have it, I blush and stiffen up. I get afraid they will laugh at me, so far none of my friends have (apart from fake ones after I stopped being their friend, I'd say). I don't really care to know if they laugh about it. It's their tough crap because someday real soon, karma will get them for finding it funny. Step 2 is to just get it out. I don't know if you will feel comfortable telling your new friends or friends you already have that you are just after being diagnosed with Tourette's. Don't beat around the bush, there's nothing like being straight and honest. If anything, they will admire you for your strength and courage. It's not easy being a person with Tourette's, and it's not easy to pluck up the courage to admit it. If you feel like you absolutely 100% cannot do it, maybe ask your parent/guardian to let your friends know the next time they come to visit. This also counts if you have known them for a while. It doesn't matter how you tell your friends, as long as you tell them. For example, your tics could end up getting bad in their home and they wouldn't know what to do because you would be to stressed to tell them properly. Make sure you know the information yourself so you can tell them what to do in every situation, and how to deal with it. Maybe if your Tourette's gets bad you like to go home. Let them know this so they can call your parent/guardian so they can collect you, or tell one of their parents/guardians so they can bring you home. Never feel you are burdening someone. If you feel like going home, GO HOME.

I know for a fact that if I ever got to the stage of needing to go home because of my tics or my panic attacks that my best friend Kimberley's mam would bring me home no problem. For these types of problems, parents/guardians need to be prepared for things like this to happen. My Tourette's is only a little over mild, but I still struggle with it at times. I've never had an attack in Kimberey's house, though, because we have too much fun (cheers, Kim!).It's so important that you  let people know in case these sort of things happen at a sleepover.

If you are a parent/guardian, I'd suggest letting the parents of your child's friends know what's going on. Sometimes, your child may be too embarrassed to tell their friends parents what's going on. Make sure you are there to do this and understand Tourette's 100% yourself.

**Medication.**

The medication I was prescribed to help ease my tics is Abilify or Aripiprazole. At first I was prescribed I think 5 mg, then I moved up to 20. Yes, my touette's was that bad at one stage. I had to take 20 mg of Abilify every day for about a year. Then I went down to 15, and stayed on 15 mg until I was finished my exams for the Leaving Certificate. Then I was brought down to 10 mg and there I remain. I hope in the future to go down to 7.5 mg as I feel I am well able. I know that Abilify can have side effects like drowsiness but it worked for me. I hope if any of you or someone you know is on this medication that it is working perfectly for you. I once read that it can increase anxiety too, but as a person suffering with anxiety I can happily say it hasn't affected it negatively at all. In fact, it actually soothes my anxiety too! So whenever my Tourette's is acting up, or I feel like I am going to have a panic attack, I take this medication and I feel better after a while. I'm just so delighted it works. To be honest I wouldn't have got very far without my medication, it has helped me while going out in public or just sitting at home. If you don't want to be on medication, I'm not sure what else can help you. Maybe talk to your doctor about it, I don't want to act like a health professional. All I can tell you is that Abilify really helped me a lot. I'm hoping to try wean myself off it, and eventually I'll be medication free.

**Overview.**

This is where I conclude my chapter on Tourette's. I remember being in therapy one day, and the lady told me a quote that will forever stay in my mind. "I have Tourette's, but Tourette's doesn't have me". I mentioned that earlier, and I will mention it always. It's important that you realize that your Tourette's doesn't define you. It's just a part of you, it doesn't control you. Never give in to it and let your life go downhill. It's not healthy and it takes a long time to heal yourself. The best advice I can possibly give is in this book. I'd suggest talking to your therapist or doctor about medication. If you or someone you know is thinking about going on medication, make sure you/they take it on the prescribed days and even if there's a certain time. I have to take min once daily, so I presume most other medications are the same. I'd highly suggest Abilify if you are thinking of it. Talk to your doctor about the risks and side effects, then decide for yourself or with a parent/guardian/partner.

# Chapter Five: Anxiety disorder.

This was the worst one for me. I struggled with it more than I did with my Tourette's. Anxiety may be defined as "a feeling of worry, nervousness or unease about something with an uncertain outcome".

## Anxiety attacks.

Anxiety attacks are truly horrible. There are many different feelings one gets when they have an anxiety attack. For me, I feel a weight on my chest, I get light headed, my thumbs become paralyzed, my face becomes numb and I sweat so much. It feels like it'll never end, and if it does it will result in you dying. I feel this way during every panic attack. You won't die, though. The worst that will happen to you is that you will pass out. Don't keep thinking that you are going to die. If you think like that, you will panic more and then pass out.

**How to calm down during a panic attack.**

This was mentioned in a previous chapter, but in case you don't have Tourette's syndrome and are only interested in this chapter, I will explain it once more. If you or anyone you know suffers from panic attacks(definition: a sudden overwhelming feeling of anxiety), read on.

Step 1. Sit on the edge of your bed. It must be your bed, because I recommend sleeping straight away afterwards. If it's daytime, take a small nap at least. Panic attacks are tiring and hard work.

Step 2. Place your hands on your stomach.

Step 3. Breathe in softly through your nose, hold for 3 seconds, then exhale through your mouth. Focus on the movement of your tummy as it goes up and down as you inhale and exhale.

Step 4. Repeat until you are completely satisfied with your breathing. Then lay down and have a good sleep/nap.

I always do this. Ever since my therapist taught me a few years back. It actually works. If your old method no longer works or if you're searching for a method, this one has got me out of a lot of "I'm going to pass out" moments. I'd suggest giving it a go, and if it doesn't work for you maybe do some research or ask your therapist for new ways to calm down during an anxiety attack.

**For people who are reading this book for someone they know: panic attacks.**

Whether you are a parent/guardian/partner or sibling, if you are present during the person's panic attacks there are a few pointers you need to know. Always have the above method (or whichever method works for person) written down and bring it when you go out. If you know it off by heart, that's even better!

If you were, say, out at a restaurant and your daughter(for example) got anxious because of all the noise and began having a panic attack, bring your daughter to the loo and ask her to sit on the toilet seat. Remain calm, don't try to force your daughter to calm down. Be patient with her. Any forceful behavior will cause your daughter to become more anxious and therefore the attack will become worse. Ask her to do her breathing exercises. Your daughter may struggle to do them at first, especially if she is crying. Remain calm, and try your best to encourage her to do her exercises. Stay in the loo with your daughter for as long as she needs to. Don't force her to leave the loo if she isn't ready to or is still feeling a little anxious. Make sure her breathing is calm, if she overheats that her cheeks have become less flushed and that she is truly ready to leave. . If your daughter manages to calm down, give her a treat. Maybe buy her that Sims game she wanted or an ice cream after she finishes her meal. Trust me, calming down during a panic attack is hard work and you need to be rewarded. As soon as you get home, put your daughter to bed. Make sure she gets a good night's sleep. That is very important.

**Dealing with Agoraphobia.**

Agoraphobia is the fear of large spaces. I have this phobia, and it is not a nice one. If you or someone you know is struggling with this phobia or think you/they might be, keep reading.

When I first started to get anxious about things, I started to hate open spaces. I couldn't stand in the P.E hall without my Tourette's acting up and my breathing. I like to know that I have something I can hold onto. I am too aware of the lack off objects around me. Even in big cities like London, or in Dublin I have to have something to hold onto (or someone). If you or someone you know has this phobia, train yourself to become aware of when that person is in a large space. Allow them to hold onto you. This will help them in ways you don't understand, but you don't have to. It's just something they are afraid of. Like some people are afraid of spiders or oranges. No phobia is ridiculous, because that's the thing they fear.

Example scenario

You and your friend are walking through the shopping mall. You decide that you would like to go to shop in your favorite store, but the gap between you and your favorite store is too wide for your liking. So you tell your friend that you need to do this slowly. All you need to do is look for an object close to you. So you see a flower pot. You link arms with your friend (or if your one of those people who is too embarrassed, you don't have to. Maybe just grab a hold of your sleeves or squeeze the side of your pockets in your hoodie or tracksuit bottoms/jeans). Then you notice that there is a cardboard cutout. You walk to that. Another flower pot. Great! Almost there! THERE WE GO! You did it! You reached your favorite store. Well done you! (Repeat the steps on the way out, too).

_____

___

This is what I do when I think the space is too big for me to reach the store. It helps EVERY TIME. It was actually my friend Kimberley who gave me this idea because one day I couldn't leave a store because the space was too wide (Thanks Kim! I owe you one). She told me to walk to the flower pot, then to Zara, then to the little cafe and I was there! Don't panic too much. That dress you seen online? That could be yours. That video game you saw was coming out? That could be yours. All it takes is to follow these little steps. You'll be fine, trust me!

**Final tip on Anxiety.**

I know having anxiety can be so super tough. Hopefully you will be able to deal with it thanks to my advice above. If you are having any trouble with my instructions, don't give up. Talk to a parent/guardian and have them do some research with you about other breathing exercises during panic attacks. For parents/guardians make sure you are 100% there for them, and have everything ready when you go out just in case. Someone can't just force a panic attack on themselves, it happens without them wanting it to! Remember this always. I know it can be frustrating, but remember: It's more frustrating for the person actually having the attack. I honestly hope the technique taught to me helps! Good luck.

**Chapter Six: Self Harm.**

This subject can be very touchy for many people. If you are easily triggered, I'd suggest maybe reading this with a parent/guardian around just in case. When I was younger, I self harmed A LOT. It felt better for me to do so. I thought I had to do it to feel better. I was so, so wrong. Don't think that self harming is the best way to relieve your pain. Believe it or not, talking to people is. I have a very good tip (taught to me by a private counsellor I had) that helps me EVERY TIME I feel like self harming (because the urge doesn't really go away sometimes).

**Self harm tips.**

My first tip (which is the one I was taught) is to get some ice (or another cold object from the freezer). Squeeze said object really tight. If you don't want to squeeze it tight, that's fine. Just squeeze it as much as you need to. Believe it or not, this method works well because it gives you the same relief as of self harming, without harming you! I find this one very useful, it works EVERY TIME. Please try it!

My second tip is to think about something/someone you truly love or do something you truly love doing. My nana and Grandaunt passed away a few years back. When I was depressed, I thought of them every day without fail. This also helped me to stop self harming. I just thought "my

Nana wouldn't be happy if she saw me doing this!" And it really helped. I also would also curl up under my blankets and watch a film(usually The Mummy at the time). Doing something you love and thinking of someone you love truly helps. If it doesn't, I'd advise trying tip one.

## Dealing with people calling you an attention seeker.

This is a very common problem. While some people do self harm to attract attention or to make themselves look 'emo', not everyone does. I remember telling a friend I self harmed (she also did once) and she gave me the impression she thought I was a fake. When in fact, I went through the horrible stages of depression for months afterwards and she was totally fine! She moved schools, made new friends and left me behind! It's these kinds of people who make it look like a joke. Don't listen to them. Seek professional help, or talk to your parents/guardians.

Even if you fear upsetting your parents/guardians, it's better than the end result! Always get help. It's always going to be okay.

**There will always be light.**

It may seem like there's no light now, but trust me..there is! It's never the end. Even death is just the beginning. Suicidal thoughts are normal when you are depressed, but never carry them out. Always get help.

To parents/guardians if your child is showing signs of depression and is self harming, bring them to a doctor immediately! Waste no time! My parents brought me to the doctor, and he admitted me to therapy sooner than I had originally been admitted. Your child needs your support and help. They feel so helpless and lost in the dark. Make sure they see the light. Make sure you reassure them it's there.

For those of you struggling with self harm, I wish you the very best of luck. I know you will get better, just like I did.

**Chapter Seven: For Everybody!**

Well, this is the final chapter of my book. I just want to say thank you for reading this book. It means a lot to me, as I have dreamt of writing this book for so long. I know it's not that long. I hope it was helpful, though.

For those of you with Asperger's: Keep being you. There's nothing wrong with being a little unusual. Absolutely nothing! I love being 'weird'. I love being me. Collect your pens and watch Star Wars ten times a day. Let the haters hate! You're great just the way you are.

For those of you with Tourette's: Don't let it define you. You are a person beyond your Tourette's. You can do many wonderful things. You CAN finish school. You CAN go to University. You CAN meet a great man and have beautiful babies. Don't let anyone tell you otherwise. You're well capable!

For those of you with Anxiety: Stay strong! It's tough, I know. Someday you'll be able to do the things you think you can't do now. You will be that dancer for Justin Timberlake. You will be in that famous movie sequel. You will sing on the x Factor and potentially win it! You just got to keep trying!

Last but not least, for ALL of you as a community. We are people. We are beautiful. I don't care how dramatic I sound. Don't ever let anyone make you feel alienated. You are part of this society. You are a strong, beautiful individual. Play the role you want to play. Thank you all for reading this book. I hope you enjoyed and will read my next few projects! Lots of love always and forever.

Don't give up little beauties. Everything will be okay. *Just Believe.*

Printed in Great Britain
by Amazon